TIME TRAVEL GUIDES

ANCIENT GREECE

Anna Claybourne

Raintree

www.raintree.co.uk/library
Visit our website to find out more information about Raintree books.

To order:
 Phone 44 (0) 1865 888112
 Send a fax to 44 (0) 1865 314091
 Visit the Raintree bookshop at www.raintree.co.uk/library to browse our catalogue and order online.

First published in Great Britain by Raintree, Halley Court, Jordan Hill, Oxford OX2 8EJ, part of Harcourt Education. Raintree is a registered trademark of Harcourt Education Ltd.

© Harcourt Education Ltd 2007
First published in paperback in 2008
The moral right of the proprietor has been asserted.

Editorial: Sarah Shannon, Lucy Beevor, and Harriet Milles
Design: Steve Mead and Geoff Ward
Picture Research: Ruth Blair
Illustrations: Eikon Illustration & Tim Slade
Production: Duncan Gilbert

Originated by Modern Age
Printed and bound in China by South China Printing Company Limited

10 digit ISBN 1 4062 0598 2 (hardback)
13 digit ISBN 978 1 4062 0598 5

11 10 09 08 07
10 9 8 7 6 5 4 3 2 1

10-digit ISBN 1 4062 0605 9 (paperback)
13-digit ISBN 978 1 4062 0605 0

11 10 09 08
10 9 8 7 6 5 4 3 2 1

British Library Cataloguing in Publication Data
Claybourne, Anna
Ancient Greece. - (Time travel guides)
1. Greece - Civilization - To 146 B.C.
938
A full catalogue record for this book is available from the British Library

Acknowledgements
The publishers would like to thank the following for permission to reproduce photographs:
AKG Images **pp. 23, 31, 49** (Eric Lessing), **32–33, 51** (John Hios), **22**; Alamy/nagelstock.com **p. 24**; Ancient Art & Architecture Collection **pp. 41** (Vatican Museum), **17, 20–21, 26–27, 36, 40, 45**; Art Archive **pp. 13** (Acropolis Museum Athens/Dagli Orti), **35** (Museo Nazionale Taranto/Dagli Orti), **38** (Archaeological Museum Naples/Dagli Orti), **28** (Archaeological Museum Florence/Dagli Orti), **48** (Archaeological Museum Piraeus/Dagli Orti), **42–43** (Archaeological Museum Volos/Dagli Orti), **6–7, 39, 52–53** (Dagli Orti), **46** (Kanellopoulos Museum Athens/Dagli Orti), **37** (Museo Nazionale Terme Rome/Dagli Orti), **24** (Agora Museum Athens/Dagli Orti), **29** (Archaeological Museum Istanbul/Dagli Orti), **47** (Musée du Louvre Paris/Dagli Orti); Corbis **pp. 10** (Jeremy Horner), **19** (Corbis/Bettmann).

Cover photograph of the Acropolis in Athens reproduced with permission of Corbis/zefa/Erika Koch. Cover photographs of ancient Greek cups reproduced with permission of Werner Forman Archive/Christies, London.

The publishers would like to thank Michael Vickers for his assistance in the preparation of this book.

Every effort has been made to contact copyright holders of any material reproduced in this book. Any omissions will be rectified in subsequent printings if notice is given to the publishers.

CONTENTS

Words that appear in the text in bold, **like this**, are explained in the Glossary.

MACEDONIA

MOUNT OLYMPUS

AEGEAN SEA

THEATRE OF DIONYSUS

ITHACA

Delphi

Chalcis

Thebes

Marathon

Athens

OLYMPIC GAMES AT OLYMPIA

Corinth

Mycenae

Argos

Olympia

Sparta

ACROPOLIS

Europe

Italy

ANCIENT GREECE

Eastern Asia

Africa

Mediterranean Sea

SEA OF CRETE

CRETE

Knossos

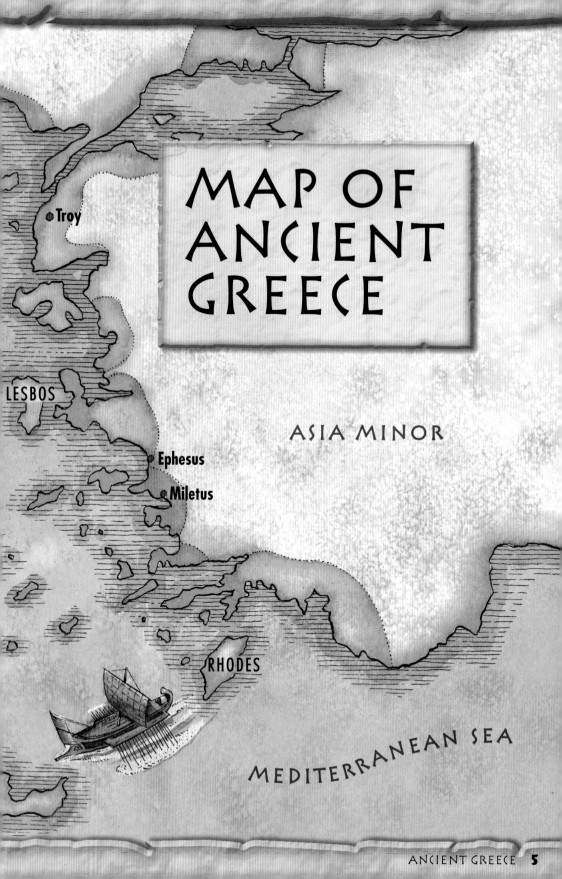

MAP OF ANCIENT GREECE

Troy

LESBOS

ASIA MINOR

Ephesus

Miletus

RHODES

MEDITERRANEAN SEA

This is Mount Parnassus, sacred to the Greek god Apollo.

CHAPTER 1

FACTS ABOUT ANCIENT GREECE

Ancient Greece is one of the ancient world's top tourist destinations. It has something for everyone – thrilling theatre, spectacular sporting events, beautiful buildings, great art, vibrant cities, and stunning landscapes. What's more, ancient Greece is a highly advanced society. It is the home of **democracy**, **philosophy**, and modern medicine. All this is combined with great weather, beautiful beaches, and fabulous food! So, step this way to find out all the facts you need to know about ancient Greece – what to do, what to wear, and what you'll eat. Our useful tips will have you feeling at home in no time!

WHEN TO TRAVEL

Ancient Greece is a great place to visit, but you should avoid certain periods if you don't want to get caught up in a bloody battle or be executed by a ruthless **tyrant**.

WAR AND WEAPONS

The ancient Greeks go to war a lot. If it's not the two great cities of Athens and Sparta doing battle, it's the Mycenaeans or the Macedonians trying to take over the rest of ancient Greece. The Greeks are also far from friendly with the Persians.

Because they fight so much, the ancient Greeks have some of the best armour, weapons, and battle **tactics** in the ancient world.

DRACO

In about 621 BC Draco was appointed to rewrite the laws of Athens. And he did — making them incredibly harsh. Draco's reign of terror lasted 27 years and gave us the word "draconian", meaning "severe" or "strict".

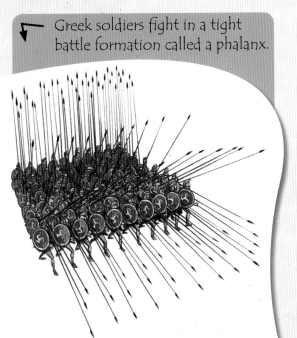

Greek soldiers fight in a tight battle formation called a phalanx.

A Greek footsoldier from the 7th century BC, called a hoplite.

ANCIENT GREEK RULERS

For most of ancient Greek history there is no one ruler. Instead, each city has its own leader or group of leaders. We recommend you visit ancient Greece around 478–430 BC. It is the golden age of ancient Greece and part of the time known as the **Classical period**. Art, learning, and culture are at their height in Athens – and there's not a spear in sight.

ANCIENT GREECE – WHEN TO VISIT

(Note: dates given are approximate.)

3000 BC	Minoans develop early culture on the island of Crete.
1450 BC	Mycenaeans grab power from the Minoans.
1250 BC	Greek armies besiege Troy in the Trojan War.
740 BC	Sparta begins attacking and conquering other cities.
650–594 BC	Tyrants and rebel leaders seize control of Athens.
621 BC	Athens suffers under the merciless laws of Draco.
546 BC	Persians begin attacking Greece and its colonies.
508 BC	Athenian leader Cleisthenes brings in democratic system.
490 BC	Greeks beat Persians at the Battle of Marathon.
478 BC	Greek cities form the Delian League to resist Persia.
449 BC	Delian League and Persia agree a peace deal.
478 BC	Athens begins "golden age" of learning, art, and culture.
445 BC	Athens makes a peace pact with its neighbour Sparta.
431–421 BC	First Peloponnesian War between Athens and Sparta.
430 BC	Deadly plague hits Athens.
413–404 BC	Sparta fights and eventually takes control of Athens.
395–387 BC	Several Greek cities and the Persians fight Sparta.
362 BC	Sparta and Athens join forces to fight Thebes.
338 BC	Macedonian king Philip II takes control of Greece.
336–323 BC	Philip's son Alexander takes power and conquers a large empire.

Key:

Stay away – danger!   Best time to visit – go for it!

Okay time to visit

GEOGRAPHY AND CLIMATE

It's no surprise that ancient Greece is a top destination for travellers. In addition to its great cities, countryside, beaches, mountains, and islands, it has lovely sunny weather. This is because ancient Greece is on the Mediterranean Sea, and has what is called a Mediterranean climate. That means it has damp winters and warm, dry summers. The surrounding sea stores heat so that the weather never gets too hot or too cold. In fact, experts think that great early **civilizations** like ancient Greece, Egypt, and Sumer grew up near the Mediterranean partly because of its warm weather. It was easy to grow crops and find shelter, so people had more time to develop other things, like art and politics.

LOCAL PRODUCE

As well as mountains and islands, Greece has plenty of rolling plains that are great for growing crops. Ancient Greek farmers mainly grow wheat and barley, along with vegetables, olive trees, and grapes for wine. They keep pigs, poultry, sheep, and goats, as well as bees for honey. There's no sugar, so honey or boiled grape juice are used as sweeteners.

EARTHQUAKES AND VOLCANOES

A visit to ancient Greece involves the risk of being shaken to bits in an earthquake or burned to a crisp in a volcanic lava flow. Greece is an earthquake and volcano zone because it lies on the boundary between three major **tectonic plates** – the huge pieces that make up the Earth's crust (hard, outer layer).

WHAT THE ANCIENT GREEKS SAY ABOUT IT...

Ancient Greek philosophers were very puzzled by earthquakes. Thales of Miletus said the Earth floated on water, and earthquakes happened when waves rocked the Earth. But Aristotle believed the wind caused earthquakes. He wrote: "A great wind is compressed into a smaller space and so gets the upper hand, and then breaks out and beats against the earth and shakes it violently."
No one in ancient Greece knew about tectonic plates, the real cause of earthquakes. They weren't discovered until the 20th century.

Mount Thera is the greatest volcano in ancient Greece. When the volcano erupted in about 1630 BC, it completely destroyed the centre of the island of Thera, leaving an enormous volcanic **crater**. The eruption was one of the most powerful in history. Ancient Greece's most famous earthquake happened in 1700 BC.
It destroyed the Minoan palace at Knossos (it was later rebuilt).

CLOTHES AND CUISINE

If you're going to blend into ancient Greek life, you'd better find yourself something to wear. You will also need to have a convincing Grecian hairstyle.

WHAT TO WEAR

If you want to dress like the locals, it's got to be a tunic, or *chiton*. Men and boys wear a short knee-length tunic, made from a piece of light wool or linen, with a belt to hold it in place. Women and girls wear longer tunics, pinned at the shoulders with brooches and wrapped around the body. If you're very rich, you might be able to afford an imported cotton or silk chiton printed with patterns. For your feet, you can buy leather shoes or sandals – though many people go barefoot.

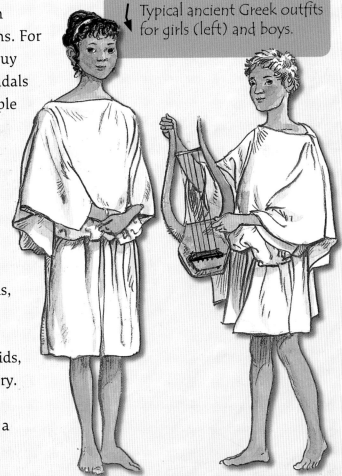

Typical ancient Greek outfits for girls (left) and boys.

HOW TO DO YOUR HAIR

Ancient Greek hair fashions depend on when you visit. In golden-age Athens, women and girls tie their hair up and decorate it with braids, ribbons, and jewellery. Most men and boys wear short hair and a trimmed beard.

WHAT'S FOR DINNER?

The main food in ancient Greece is porridge or bread made from wheat or barley. Everyone eats this all the time. Fruit and vegetables eaten in ancient Greece include figs, apples, pears, plums, cherries, onions, peas, carrots, spinach, garlic, squashes, and beans – and there is always plenty of olive oil. Thanks to Greece's miles of coastline, there is also plenty of fresh fish, such as octopus. Meat and vegetables can be expensive, so the ancient Greeks go out and hunt hares, deer, and pigeons, or collect their own mushrooms and berries. To drink, everyone has wine mixed with water – even the children! Dessert is usually fruit or honey cake.

This carving clearly shows a young woman's braided, decorated hairstyle from about 500 BC.

HONEY CAKE

This is Chrysippus of Tyana's recipe for *gastris*, a type of honey cake from the island of Crete:

- Mix 1½ cups of ground sesame seeds with 1 cup of warmed honey to make dough. Divide it into two pieces and roll them out into large flat cakes, using an oiled rolling pin.
- Grind 3 cups of mixed nuts and a handful of poppy seeds, and mix with half a cup of warm olive oil. Spread the mixture on one piece of dough, and top with the other piece.
- Leave to set for an hour, cut into slices, and serve with fruit.

CULTURE AND CUSTOMS

You will have a better time in ancient Greece if you know how society works. You'll need to understand the difference between a **citizen** and a slave, for a start. And remember that the ancient Greeks haven't heard of equal rights for men and women.

CITIZENS

A citizen is a full member of society, who can vote and own property. In Athens, most citizens are men who were born there. People from outside Athens, called *metics*, are sometimes made into citizens, but it's very rare.

WOMEN

In ancient Greece, women belong to their male relatives. You can be a "citizen woman" if you're related to a citizen – but you still have no rights and you can't vote. Wealthy women have to stay indoors and run the house. Poorer women might work in the fields or in the market. Either way, unlike boys, most girls don't go to school or learn to read and write.

WHAT THE ANCIENT GREEKS SAY ABOUT IT...

"Teaching a woman to read and write? What a terrible thing to do! Like feeding a vile snake on more poison."
[Athenian writer Menander (342–291 BC) gives a **sexist** ancient Greek view. Unfortunately it was normal for the ancient Greeks to treat women as less important than men.]

However, things are a little different in war-loving Sparta. There, women can own property and girls learn to read and write. In Sparta, women are seen as important because they become mothers to the next generation of soldiers. So, women are encouraged to become physically strong by running and other sports, so that they will be healthy and able to bear strong children.

RICH AND POOR

Just like many modern cities, ancient Greek cities such as Athens have a super-rich upper class and a very poor **underclass**. Life is very different depending on whether you're a wealthy politician, an **architect**, a writer, or a poor farmer, builder, or **artisan**.

SLAVES

Greek culture is run on slave labour. Slaves do all the hard work like farming, mining, and building. There are also household slaves who do the housework. Slaves can be male or female, and some become slaves as children. Prisoners from other lands, criminals, and runaways often end up becoming slaves.

↑ A well-dressed, wealthy ancient Greek woman with her slave.

DON'T BE RUDE!

Manners matter in ancient Greece. The great Greek poet Hesiod, who lived around 700 BC, wrote a list of good manners. Here are some to remember:

- Always wash your hands before drinking a toast to the gods.
- Don't go to the toilet in the street!
- Never laugh at people for being poor. It's not their fault.
- It's the height of rudeness to cut your fingernails at a feast.

COMMUNICATIONS

In ancient Greece there are no phones and there's certainly no Internet. To send a message, you have to use a messenger, so news travels slowly.

CODED MESSAGES

In times of war, the ancient Greeks send secret messages so that important information can't fall into the wrong hands. One way is to tattoo the message on to the messenger's shaved head then send him once his hair has grown. The messenger shaves his head again to reveal the message!

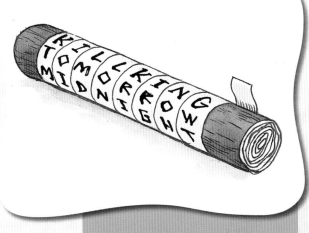

Wrapped around a scytale, a strip of letters reveals a secret message.

The Spartans use another cunning method. They send messages written on long strips of leather. They look like nonsense unless you know how to decode the message – by wrapping it around a stick of exactly the right size, called a **scytale**. The letters then line up and form words.

RELIGION

The ancient Greeks have many gods, and they are very important to everyday life. You'll see temples, altars, and statues of gods everywhere in ancient Greece.

GODS AND GODDESSES

There are dozens of ancient Greek gods and goddesses. Here are a few of the most important:

- **Zeus** – king of the gods and the father of many of the younger gods.
- **Hera** – Zeus's wife, and goddess of women and marriage.
- **Athena** – goddess of war and wisdom; she also guards over Athens.
- **Apollo** – god of the Sun and light; prayed to by artists and musicians.
- **Artemis** – twin sister of Apollo and the goddess of the Moon and of hunting.
- **Dionysus** – god of wine, parties, and the theatre; famous for his fun-loving ways.
- **Demeter** – goddess of the Earth, plants, and farming.
- **Aphrodite** – goddess of love and beauty; she is beautiful and very vain.
- **Asclepius** – god of medicine; a human doctor made into a god by Zeus.
- **Poseidon** – god of the sea, and Zeus's brother; known for his terrible temper.
- **Pluto** – god of the Underworld, where souls wander after death.
- **Hermes** – messenger of the gods, and the god of travel.

A GOD FOR EVERY OCCASION

Different ancient Greek gods have different jobs to do. For example, Zeus is the king of the gods, his daughter Athena is the goddess of war, and Hermes is the messenger of the gods. The gods can control events, do magic, change shape, and answer prayers. Watch out though – ancient Greek gods are not always good, kind, and caring. They can be jealous and cruel, and will get back at you if you annoy them.

This vase painting dated 520 BC shows Dionysus, god of wine and parties!

STORIES OF THE GODS

The ancient Greeks have hundreds of stories about their gods, which they tell in the form of **tapestries**, decorated silverware, vase paintings, carvings, poems, and plays. These stories are an important part of Greek **mythology**.

One Greek myth tells the story of a beauty competition between the goddesses Aphrodite, Athena, and Hera, which was judged by Paris, prince of Troy. Aphrodite won the competition by promising Paris the most beautiful woman in the world – Helen, a Greek queen. But when Paris stole Helen away, the Trojan War began (see also page 39).

PRAYER AND WORSHIP

Many temples and religious festivals are dedicated to particular gods. One of ancient Greece's biggest and best religious festivals is the Panathenaea. It's held every year in Athens in the late summer, to celebrate the birthday of the goddess Athena. Like most ancient Greek religious festivals, it features feasts, processions, music, sports, and **sacrifices** of food and wine.

WHAT THE ANCIENT GREEKS SAY ABOUT IT...

"So spoke the goddess, flashing-eyed Athena, and she departed in the likeness of a sea-eagle; and amazement fell upon all at the sight."

[The poet Homer, who lived around 800 BC, describes the goddess Athena changing shape in his great poem *The Odyssey*.]

Many ancient Greeks have an altar in their courtyard at home, where they make offerings – such as a *libation*, which means pouring wine onto the altar. At feasts, some of the food is sacrificed to the gods. If you have a question for one of the gods, you can visit a special **shrine** called an **oracle**.

Part of the oracle of Apollo at Delphi, where people from Athens leave their offerings to the god.

ASK THE ORACLE

When you visit an oracle, enter the oracle temple and ask your question. (Common questions include things like "Should I go to Kos next week?" or "Is Zeus angry with me?") The priestess may go into a **trance** or look into the flames of a holy fire for the answer. Or you may have to stay the night in the temple and wait for the god to speak to you in a dream.

A 21st-century view of the beautiful Parthenon temple, the most famous building in Athens.

CHAPTER 2

GOVERNMENT AND POLITICS

Ancient Greece, especially Athens, is famous for its advanced government. The ancient Greek political system still influences the way we do things in the 21st century! During its golden age in the 5th century BC, ancient Greece is not a single country with one king or queen. Instead, it's made up of lots of '**city-states**'. A city-state is a city, such as Athens, Argos, or Mycenae, along with the villages and countryside around it. Each city-state has its own rulers and laws, so don't forget where you are. What is allowed in Athens could be a crime in Sparta!

ANCIENT GREECE **21**

ALL ABOUT ATHENS

Athens is the jewel in ancient Greece's crown. A centre of learning, art, and culture, and a major military power, it's the most important of all the city-states. It's a top destination for the artists, writers, scientists, and philosophers who come here from all over the Mediterranean.

Athens has a long history – in fact it has probably been a town since prehistoric times. By 440 BC it has become the most powerful city in ancient Greece. Athens started as a small settlement, possibly around 1400 BC. The first Athenians lived on top of a high hill. This was the safest place to watch out for enemies, and there was also a spring providing fresh water. Gradually, the rest of the city grew around this hilltop area, which became known as the Acropolis.

A sunset view of the Acropolis in Athens as it looks today, with its temples and ancient walls.

TAKING CONTROL

Over the centuries, Athens won a lot of battles against other city-states. It also grew rich, thanks to its local silver mines and the fertile plains around it, and became a centre for travel and trade. All this added to Athens' power and its free-thinking culture.

THE NAMING OF ATHENS

Athens is named after the goddess Athena. According to ancient Greek legend, Athena, goddess of war and wisdom, and Poseidon, god of the sea, both wanted to be the god of the city. So they each offered the people a gift. Athena's gift was an olive tree and Poseidon's was a well. Unfortunately, the well's water was as salty as the sea. So the people decided Athena's gift was far more useful, and she became the city's goddess.

An engraving showing the statue of Athena inside the Parthenon.

ATHENS FACTS

- **Population in 440 BC**: about 300,000
- **Percentage of population who are citizens**: about 15 per cent
- **Nearest port**: Piraeus
- **Highest point**: on top of the Acropolis – 150 metres (510 feet) above sea level

HANGING OUT

Around Athens you'll find theatres, libraries, **gymnasiums** (leisure centres), public baths, shops, and stalls. Everywhere you go you'll find the free-thinking citizens discussing their leaders, the latest wars, political decisions, the plays they've seen, and the parties they've been to.

THE ACROPOLIS

Most city-states have an **acropolis**. It's usually the oldest part of town, and acts as a refuge in times of war. Athens' acropolis is the most famous of all. It's full of temples, mainly devoted to the goddess Athena, such as the Parthenon, and statues, such as the "Athena Parthenos".

DEMOCRACY

Some city-states are ruled by tyrants or kings. But since about 500 BC, there's a new system in Athens, called democracy. It means rule by the people – from the Greek words *demos* meaning "people" and *kratos* meaning "power".

However, Athenian democracy is not true democracy as only citizens can vote – that is, free men who were born in Athens.

SPARTA

Sparta is the opposite of its arch-enemy, Athens. Don't go there unless you're hard as nails! While the Athenians are into art, culture, and parties, the Spartans only care about fighting. They train their children to be tough fighters by beating them and forcing them to fend for themselves.

This means that many people are left out, including women and slaves. As a visitor to Athens, you won't be allowed to vote. But don't despair! If you do a great deed for the city, such as winning a battle, you could be made a citizen of Athens as a reward.

DIRECT DEMOCRACY

In ancient Greek democracy, the citizens can also take part in decisions. They just turn up to a big public meeting, called the **Assembly**, and vote on new laws or on things like whether money should be spent on warships or a new temple. In Athens there have to be at least 600 citizens at the Assembly to vote. People vote by holding up their hand or a stick.

OSTRAKA

If you find bits of broken tortoiseshell or pottery lying about with names scrawled on them, you've stumbled across some *ostraka*. Once a year, the citizens get to vote on any politicians they think should be kicked out. They write their names on ostraka, and then all the votes are counted.

Greeks enjoy gathering in public places to listen to speakers.

This picture of a Greek warship powered by oarsmen was painted in around 500 BC.

CHAPTER 3

TRAVEL, FOOD, AND SHELTER

Ancient Greece is a big place, and you'll probably use several forms of transport on your travels. Luckily the wheel has been invented, so **chariots**, carts, and wagons are common. And the ancient Greeks certainly know what they're doing when it comes to sea travel – they're master shipbuilders and top-notch **navigators**. If you're lucky, you'll be invited to stay in someone's house too, so you'll find out how the ancient Greeks live.

ON THE MOVE

The number one form of transport in ancient Greece is walking. Most people can't afford anything else. There are no cars, bikes, buses, or trams, so in cities you'll have to go on foot.

TRAVEL BY LAND

Like most ancient cultures, the ancient Greeks rely a lot on horses, donkeys, and asses. Horses were first tamed in central Asia, around 3000 BC. By 1000 BC, they are being used in ancient Greece. However, only the very wealthy can afford to keep a horse.

If you can afford it, you can ride in a horse-drawn carriage or chariot. Or, if you're confident enough, you can just ride the horse itself. But there are no saddles, just blankets and reins. (Riding is considered the tough, manly option.) And if you're on a budget, you could try hitching a free ride on a farmer's ox or donkey wagon.

A VERY LONG RUN

In 490 BC, according to legend, a messenger ran all the way from Marathon to Athens — a journey of about 42 kilometres (26 miles) — with the news that the Greeks had won the Battle of Marathon against the Persians. As soon as he delivered the news, the messenger dropped dead from exhaustion! The modern marathon race is named after this story.

A vase painting showing a horse-drawn chariot in a wedding procession.

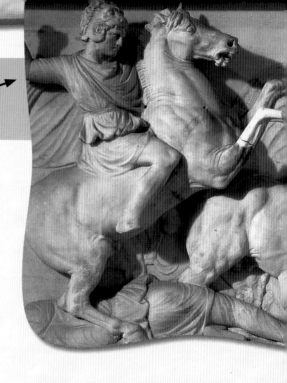

A carving on Alexander the Great's tomb shows him riding his horse bareback into battle.

TRAVEL TIPS

Follow these handy travel tips and you'll stay safe on the road.

- Avoid travelling during wars – you could get caught in the crossfire.
- For long treks, take a walking stick and a little stool for a rest.
- There are no streetlights, so at night you'll need a torch made of a stick with flaming oil at the top.
- Watch out for bandits who lie in wait for travellers and rob them.

TRAVEL BY SEA

The quickest way to travel in ancient Greece is definitely by boat. If there's a choice, ancient Greeks travel from one place to another around the coast. They also use ships to travel between the Greek islands and across the Mediterranean Sea to other lands. For a small fare, you can sail from one place to another as a passenger. For example, the trip from Piraeus (the port near Athens) to the nearby island of Aegina is about 2 obols – the same as a theatre ticket. The fare from Egypt to the Black Sea (including luggage) is 2 **drachmas**. (See page 44 for a guide to ancient Greek currency.)

Ships are powered by sails, rowers, or both. The ancient Greeks have developed highly advanced ships over centuries of exploring, trading, and holding sea battles.

WHERE TO STAY

On long journeys, you may be able to stay in guesthouses by the roadside, though they're not very fancy. There are usually inns near oracles and temples to cater for visitors. At festivals people shelter under temporary tents. Luckily for you, though, the ancient Greeks believe it's polite to offer food and shelter to any traveller who needs it, so you'll probably get to stay in someone's house.

WHAT THE ANCIENT GREEKS SAY ABOUT IT...

"My conscience would not let me turn away a stranger... for strangers and beggars all come in Zeus's name."
Eumaeus, a character in Homer's poem *The Odyssey*, explains that it is a Greek's duty to welcome strangers.

A view inside a typical ancient Greek house.

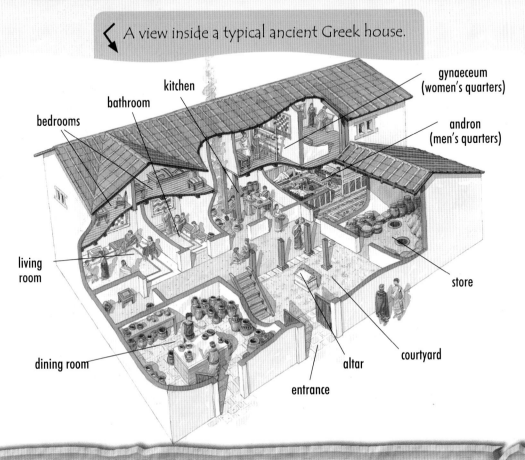

bedrooms

bathroom

kitchen

gynaeceum
(women's quarters)

andron
(men's quarters)

living
room

store

dining room

altar

courtyard

entrance

STEP INSIDE

A typical ancient Greek house is **terraced** and built of mud bricks. There are two floors, made up of rooms surrounding a central courtyard. There's a special dining room for the men, called the *andron*, and other rooms for women and slaves. The bedrooms are usually upstairs and are reached by a ladder or staircase.

Vase painting showing a slave playing the flute for a party guest.

MAKE YOURSELF AT HOME

You'll find plenty of modern conveniences in the average ancient Greek house. Bedrooms have cosy beds with proper mattresses and pillows, as well as washbasins for keeping clean. In some houses there is even a bathroom on the ground floor with a clay bathtub.

Most households have slaves, who will serve you food, wash your clothes, and even play you some music. When you leave, it is polite to give your host a thank-you gift, such as a silver bowl.

MALE AND FEMALE BEHAVIOUR

The way you'll be expected to behave while you're staying in an ancient Greek house depends whether you're male or female. For example, men and boys sit back and have everything done for them by slaves or women. Women and girls do some weaving, a bit of housework, or look after babies.

The Odeum, a 5,000-seater theatre in Athens. Going to the theatre is a favourite pastime in ancient Greece.

THINGS TO DO IN ANCIENT GREECE

There is so much to do in ancient Greece, you'll never be bored. Whether you like plays or sports – whether you like to go exploring or just prefer to relax – ancient Greece has it all. You'll find theatre, art, architecture, literature, ancient ruins, public baths, islands, and beaches... it's a time-travelling tourist's paradise.

THE THEATRE

The ancient Greeks love going to the theatre – and so they should. They invented it! It's the ultimate ancient Greek experience, so make sure you see a show while you're here.

BOOK NOW!

Plays are shown during the day, when it is still light. Performances can be long, with three plays shown one after another. You buy your tickets at the theatre as you go in. "Tickets" are bronze or lead tokens, stamped with a letter to show where to sit. Children can go to the theatre, too – but only boys. If you're a girl, you'll have to try sneaking a look from outside, as ancient Greek theatres are open-air.

GREEK THEATRES

Athens has the most famous theatre in ancient Greece – the Theatre of Dionysus. It is built into the side of the hill leading up to the Acropolis, and can seat up to 17,000 people.

Layout of a typical Greek theatre.

WHAT TO EXPECT

Greek theatre grew from old religious rituals, when a **chorus** would sing about gods and heroes. A typical ancient Greek play now has a chorus and three actors (all male), who each play several parts. Most plays are **tragedies**, which retell old legends; or comedies, which mock famous politicians or members of Greek society. (So you'll need to know a lot about ancient Greece to see the funny side.) If you can, try to see something by one of the great playwrights – Aeschylus, Sophocles, Euripides, and Aristophanes. They were all alive between 550 and 350 BC.

As Greek theatres are so big, the view from the back is dreadful. To solve this problem the actors wear exaggerated masks like these, which clearly show the emotions of the characters.

Here's a programme guide to two typical Greek plays:

- *Agamemnon* – a tragedy by Aeschylus. Greek hero and battle leader, Agamemnon, returns from the Trojan War only to be gruesomely murdered by his wife, Clytemnestra.

- *The Wasps* – a comedy by Aristophanes about an old man who loves trials so much, he puts his dog on trial for stealing some cheese.

AESCHYLUS

Aeschylus (525–456 BC) is regarded as the father of ancient Greek theatre. He wrote nearly 90 plays, winning several prizes. He was the first playwright to write for two actors, instead of just a chorus. He also liked to create special effects, such as making actors fly around using ropes.

THE OLYMPIC GAMES

For centuries, the ancient Greeks have held races and competitions as part of religious festivals. From the 8th century BC, they've held several major sports tournaments. The biggest is the Olympic Games, which is held every four years.

A 21st century view of the stade, or running track, at Olympus.

GOING TO THE GAMES

The Olympic Games are held at Olympia, which is about 325 kilometres (200 miles) from Athens. Everyone will be heading that way, so you won't get lost. In fact, the games are so important that wars are put on hold during them, to allow people to travel safely.

The Olympic Games last five days, with many different kinds of sports to watch. Ancient Greeks don't do team sports like football. Instead, individual athletes take part in foot races, chariot races, jumping contests, and throwing events such as discus and javelin.

OLYMPIC EVENTS

- **Foot race** – running up and down a track called a *stade*. (The word "stadium" comes from *stade*.)
- **Wrestling** – two wrestlers try to force each other to the ground. The winner is the first to force his opponent to fall three times.
- **Pankration** – an extra-rough form of wrestling where you're allowed to strangle your opponent, sometimes to death! Boys take part as well as men.
- **Discus** – throwing a very heavy lead, bronze, iron, or stone disc.
- **Javelin** – throwing a spear. It has to hit the ground point-first to count.
- **Chariot race** – long races for chariots drawn by two or four horses.
- **Pentathlon** – a contest of five events: foot race, long jump, discus, javelin, and wrestling.

GAMES FOR WOMEN

Women can't take part in the proper Olympics, but there's a separate sports contest for women called the *Heraea*. Married women are not allowed to watch the men's games either, but younger girls can – it is seen as a good place to meet a husband.

POINTS MEAN PRIZES

Each winning athlete gets a prize of a wreath of **laurels**. This is seen as a great honour. When a triumphant athlete returns home after the games, he usually receives a big cash reward from his city-state. However, if an athlete is caught cheating at the games, he is publicly whipped.

A sculpture of an athlete about to throw the discus.

THE HISTORY TRAIL

Greeks in the golden age of Athens (about 475–430 BC) love to look back on the even more ancient past, which they see as a time of magic and mystery. So hit the history trail to find out about the earliest Greeks of all.

THE MYSTERIOUS MINOANS

Head for Crete, Greece's largest island, to see the ruins left by the Minoans. They lived on Crete from about 2000–1100 BC and built a huge palace at Knossos. There you can see amazing frescoes (wall paintings) showing their lifestyle. The ancient Greeks tell many stories about Minos, the legendary King of Crete (see box).

A Roman mosiac showing the Greek hero Theseus wrestling with the Minotaur.

LEGEND OF THE MINOTAUR

Greek legend says that the Minotaur, a monster with a man's body and a bull's head, lived beneath the palace at Knossos in a great labyrinth or maze. Every nine years, King Minos forced the people of Athens to send seven boys and seven girls for the Minotaur to eat – until Theseus, the prince of Athens, went to Crete and killed the Minotaur.

THE MIGHTY MYCENAEANS

From about 1500 BC, a people called the Mycenaeans came to power. They were great warriors and took over large parts of ancient Greece. Mycenae, on the Greek mainland, was their capital city, but it eventually fell into ruins. These ruins are fascinating to the later ancient Greeks.

They see the Mycenaeans as legendary heroes, and they feature in many ancient Greek myths and legends.

The ruins of graves at Mycenae, home of the Mycenaeans.

TROY

The greatest ancient Greek legend of all tells how, in Mycenaean times, Paris, prince of Troy, ran away with Helen, a Greek queen. To win her back, the Greeks sailed to Troy and laid **siege** to the city for 10 years, finally destroying it. Because of these old stories, especially the work of the great Greek poet Homer and the ruins of Troy (in what is now Turkey), the ancient Greeks believe the Trojan War did really happen, in about 1200 BC.

MORE THINGS TO DO

GO TO THE GYM

If you're male, you can while away many happy hours at the gymnasium. Men go there to exercise, bathe, relax, and chat with friends. There are spaces for public baths, running, and sports training, as well as rooms for making speeches and discussing important issues.

ISLAND-HOPPING

There's more to ancient Greece than Athens and the mainland. For a change of scene, why not tour the Greek islands? They include:

- Naxos, famous for its wine and beautiful marble
- Ithaca, the home of the legendary hero Odysseus
- Chios, thought to be the birthplace of the great poet Homer.

ART AND ARCHITECTURE

Be sure to plan your visit for after ancient Greece's top buildings have been built:

- Temple of Zeus, Olympia, built around 465 BC. A great Doric temple (see following page).
- The Parthenon, Athens, built 447–432 BC. The ultimate Greek temple, dedicated to the goddess Athena.
- The Erechtheum, Athens, built around 410 BC. An elegant temple, possibly built in honour of the mythical king Erechtheus.

Corinthian columns on a temple in Athens.

KNOW YOUR COLUMNS!

Greek temples often have columns at the front or all around the outside. There are three styles:

- Doric columns have a plain rim, or "capital", at the top.
- Ionic columns have a curly, decorated capital.
- Corinthian columns are much rarer. Their capitals have carved leaf shapes all around them.

| Doric | Ionic | Corinthian |

The three types of ancient Greek columns.

GAMES AND TOYS

Ancient Greeks, both children and adults, often pass the time playing games like dice, juggling, draughts, and marbles. Knucklebones is another favourite (see box right).

LET'S PLAY KNUCKLEBONES!

- Get some knucklebones (small animal bones).
- Put five knucklebones on the ground.
- Pick up one, throw it in the air, and before catching it, quickly pick up another.
- Throw both knucklebones in the air while you pick up a third, and so on.

Can you pick up all five bones without dropping any?

This famous vase painting shows legendary Greek heroes Achilles and Ajax having a game of draughts.

A pair of ancient Greek gold earrings from about 400 BC.

CHAPTER 5

SHOPPING

When you're tired of watching plays, trekking around beautiful buildings, admiring statues, and cheering at chariot races, why not hit the shops? There are plenty of things to buy in ancient Greece's many markets. As well as the beautiful jewellery, silver, and pottery vases that the ancient Greeks make themselves, there are all the things their traders import from abroad, such as perfume bottles, ivory, and precious stones.

THE MARKETPLACE

Every town and city has a marketplace, where farmers, traders, and craftsmen bring their goods to sell. The market isn't just a place to buy things – it's the heart of city life, where people go to meet friends, gossip, have a snack, or make an announcement.

WHAT THE ANCIENT GREEKS SAY ABOUT IT...

"...crowds are surging under the market porticos [columns], encumbered with wheat that is being measured, wine-skins, oar-leathers, garlic, olives, onions in nets."
[A description of the marketplace from Aristophanes' play *The Acharnians* written in about 425 BC.]

SEE YOU AT THE AGORA

In most towns, the market is held in the *agora*, the big, flat, open central square. The agora usually has statues in the middle, and the traders set up their stalls all around the sides. In some cities there's also a *stoa* – a stone building specially designed for trading. It has columns at the front and space for a row of shops inside in the cool shade (perfect for fish and cheese stalls!).

SLAVES FOR SALE

Most agoras have a platform called a *kykloi*, where slaves are bought and sold. The price of a slave depends on how young, healthy, and useful he or she is. It can be anything up to 500 drachmas. As well as slaves, workers gather at the market to offer themselves for hire.

GREEK CURRENCY

Here's a guide to Greek currency for when you go shopping. The basic unit is the drachma. In 440 BC a skilled worker might earn about 1 drachma a day.

1 drachma = 6 obols	100 drachmas = 1 mina
1 obol = 12 chalkoi	60 minas = 1 talent

HUNGRY?

Just like in a modern mall, the market has stalls selling drinks and snacks. You can buy fruit or hot food such as honey pancakes.

WOMEN AT WORK

The market is one of the few places in ancient Greece where you'll see women out of doors and doing a job. While richer women are expected to keep house, peasant women can often be seen running market stalls.

COINS

The ancient Greeks began using coins in about 600 BC. Each city-state issues its own coins, stamped with images. Banks can get your money changed into local coins, so make sure you visit one before you head for the market! If you can't find any pockets in your tunic, do what the Greeks do and simply carry your loose change in your mouth.

A silver coin from ancient Athens, decorated with an image of the goddess Athena.

WHAT THE ANCIENT GREEKS SAY ABOUT IT...

"I fell on the ground so hard, I swallowed my money and two of my teeth." [From Aristophanes' comedy *The Birds*.]

WHAT TO BUY

You can find all kinds of things for sale in the marketplace, such as food, wine, tools, vases, jewellery, and perfumes. You will also be able to buy local silverware from the silver mines near Athens. Pick up the right souvenir and it could be worth thousands when you return to the 21st century!

FRESH FOOD

The ancient Greeks come to the marketplace mainly to buy their food. There's plenty of wheat and barley, fresh fruit and vegetables, cheese, olive oil, honey, herbs, fish, meat, and salt. Some animals, such as chickens, are sold alive.

EVERYDAY ITEMS

Clothes stalls sell *chitons* (tunics), cloaks, and sandals. The ancient Greeks also make their own clothes at home, so market traders sell raw materials such as wool and cotton. Craftsmen sell all kinds of everyday items that they've made, such as tools, lamps, jewellery, furniture, and toys.

A terracotta (pottery) ancient Greek toy soldier on horseback.

TOYS

Look out for toys to bring home for your little brother or sister. There are rattles for babies, dolls, hobby horses, spinning tops, kites, yoyos, hoops, and pottery toy animals. You can also get toy carts with mini-harnesses, to attach them to a real dog or goat!

PICK UP A POT

For a 21st-century time-traveller, the best souvenir of ancient Greece is a beautiful painted vase or pot. Even everyday pots, used for carrying water or holding wine or olive oil, can be decorated with amazing scenes of festivals, mythical heroes, gods, monsters, or sporting contests. Others are covered with intricate patterns, usually in a combination of black, white, and orange or red colours.

An ancient Greek aryballos with a female face. Aryballos are small perfume jars.

POTTERY GUIDE

The ancient Greeks use many different types of pots, jars, and vases. Before buying, make sure you know your pots with our at-a-glance guide:
- **Amphora** – storage jar for wine, oil, water, etc.
- **Stamnos, Pelike** – general storage jars.
- **Krater** – open-necked vase for holding drink during a meal.
- **Oinochoe** – jug for wine and water.
- **Skyphos, Kantharos** – drinking cups.
- **Hydria** – jar for collecting water.
- **Aryballos** – small perfume jar.

STAYING SAFE

While you're enjoying your ancient Greek trip, don't forget to look after yourself. Greece may be the most advanced civilization in the ancient world, but there are still diseases and plagues, and bandits and pickpockets on the loose.

A carving showing Asclepius, the god of medicine, caring for a patient.

VISITING THE DOCTOR

The human body is very important to the ancient Greeks. They think it's vital to be fit and healthy and to do lots of exercise (which explains their love of sport).

THE GOD OF MEDICINE

PLAGUE HORROR

Whatever you do, avoid Athens between 430–426 BC. During this time it is overrun by a terrible attack of the **plague**. No one knows how to cure it, so a quarter of the population gets wiped out!

The earliest ancient Greeks thought illnesses were caused by the gods, and only the gods could cure them. If you were ill, you prayed to Asclepius, the god of medicine, to ask him to help you. Then, if you were cured, it was polite to leave a thank-you offering to Asclepius, consisting of a picture or sculpture of the body part that was fixed.

ANCIENT GREEK MEDICINE

People still pray to Asclepius, but in the golden age (around 475–430 BC), ancient Greece also has doctors and medicines. If you're ill, you can go to a health centre called an *asclepieum*. For medicines, the Greeks use plants, such as nettles to cleanse the blood and mustard to kill germs. They also use bloodletting. This means cutting the skin to let out excess blood, which is (mistakenly) believed to cure many illnesses. The Greeks can bandage wounds and even do operations to amputate limbs. However, there's no **anaesthetic**, so try not to get ill in the first place.

TREATING A BATTLE WOUND

"He laid him at full length and cut out the sharp arrow from his thigh; he washed the black blood from the wound with warm water; he then crushed a bitter herb, rubbing it between his hands, and spread it upon the wound; this was a virtuous [good] herb which killed all pain; so the wound presently dried and the blood left off flowing..."
[A passage from Homer's *Iliad*, dating from around 800 BC.]

HIPPOCRATES – THE MOST FAMOUS DOCTOR IN ANCIENT GREECE

Unlike the doctors before him, Hippocrates (460–377 BC) believed that diseases had natural causes, instead of being caused by the gods. He used medicines, and was the first to realize that a good diet, rest, exercise, and clean air helped people to stay healthy. Hippocrates started a medical school on his home island of Cos. He made his students swear the Hippocratic oath, promising not to harm their patients. Doctors still swear the Hippocratic oath today.

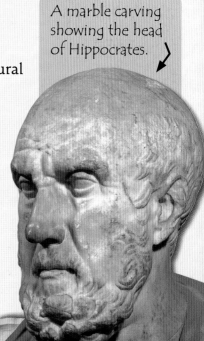
A marble carving showing the head of Hippocrates.

CRIME AND PUNISHMENT

Take care! In the ancient world, with no CCTV and no burglar alarms, it's easy for villains to commit crimes.

CATCHING CRIMINALS

There are not many police in ancient Greece. For small crimes, it is left to the citizens to catch the offender and decide on a punishment – so if your bag gets stolen, just ask someone for help. However, Athens does have a small police force made up of slaves, and there are some government officials who can arrest people for more serious crimes.

Here are some typical ancient Greek criminals to watch out for:

- Bandits wait by the roadside and rob lonely travellers. Sometimes they kill them too!
- Pirates attack ships, beat up the crew, and steal the cargo.
- Murderers – with no police force, ancient Greeks sometimes take revenge for crimes by murdering each other. Angry slaves sometimes kill their owners, too.
- Temple robbers steal precious treasures and carvings from temples.

THE TRIAL OF SOCRATES

Socrates (469–399 BC) was a great Greek philosopher who lived in the golden age of Athens. He had many young followers who listened to his teachings. Socrates' style was to ask questions about religion, politics, and right and wrong. His questions made his followers doubt the power of the state and the gods. For this, Socrates was put on trial in Athens, accused of corrupting young people and not believing in the gods. He was found guilty and sentenced to death by drinking hemlock, a poisonous plant.

ANCIENT GREEK LAW COURTS

Some ancient Greek city-states, especially Athens, have laws and law-courts to try to punish wrongdoers. Anyone suspected of a crime can be taken to court and put on trial. A law court has **magistrates**, called *arkhons*, and a **jury** made up of several hundred citizens. People are picked for jury service by selecting bronze balls from a machine called a *kleroterion*. There are no lawyers – the suspect and the person who is bringing him or her to court make their own speeches and call their own witnesses. The jurors vote using bronze voting tokens – solid for innocent and hollow for guilty.

PUNISHMENTS

Punishments for crimes include fines, being denied citizenship, being made a slave, banishment from the city, or the death penalty. The death penalty can be carried out in several horrible ways, including poisoning, being stoned to death, *apotympanismos* (being beaten to death with sticks), or being thrown off a cliff.

The voting token on the left has a solid centre, meaning "not guilty"; the one on the right, with a hollow centre, means "guilty".

Ancient Greek lettering carved into a gravestone.

CHAPTER 6

ANCIENT GREECE FACTS AND FIGURES

Like all good guide books, this one has a handy reference section at the back! Use it to learn how to read the Greek alphabet and pronounce Greek words, look up famous Greeks, and brush up on ancient Greek history at a glance.

THE GREEK CALENDAR
DAYS OF THE WEEK

The Greeks have a seven-day-week, which they copied from another great early civilization, the Sumerians. The days are named after the Sun, the Moon, and five Greek gods. The seven days are:

Hemera heliou	Day of the Sun	Sunday
Hemera selenes	Day of the Moon	Monday
Hemera Areos	Day of Ares	Tuesday
Hemera Hermu	Day of Hermes	Wednesday
Hemera Dios	Day of Zeus	Thursday
Hemera Aphrodites	Day of Aphrodite	Friday
Hemera Khronu	Day of Cronos	Saturday

MONTHS OF THE YEAR

The ancient Greek calendar has twelve months, but they have different names in different parts of Greece. This calendar shows the names used in Athens:

Hekatombaion	June/July
Metageitnion	July/August
Boedromion	August/September
Pyanepsion	September/October
Maimakterion	October/November
Poseideion	November/December
Gamelion	December/January
Anthesterion	January/February
Elaphebolion	February/March
Munychion	March/April
Thargelion	April/May

ANCIENT GREECE PHRASE BOOK

THE GREEK ALPHABET

The ancient Greek alphabet has 24 letters. This guide shows you each letter, its name, and how to pronounce it. As with modern letters, each letter has a lower-case (small) and an upper-case (capital) version.

Letter	Name of letter	Pronunciation
α	alpha	*a* as in c<u>a</u>t
β	beta	*b* as in <u>b</u>ath
γ	gamma	*g* as in goat
δ	delta	*d* as in <u>d</u>og
ε	epsilon	*e* as in b<u>e</u>d
ζ	zeta	*z* as in <u>z</u>oo
η	eta	*ay* as in d<u>ay</u>
θ	theta	*th* as in <u>th</u>ink
ι	iota	*i* as in b<u>i</u>n
κ	kappa	*k* as in <u>k</u>itchen
λ	lambda	*l* as in <u>l</u>eg
μ	mu	*m* as in <u>m</u>at
ν	nu	*n* as in <u>n</u>ose
ξ	xi	*ks* as in fo<u>x</u>
ο	omicron	*o* as in h<u>o</u>t
π	pi	*p* as in <u>p</u>ig
ρ	rho	rolled *r* as in <u>r</u>abbit
σ	sigma	*s* as in <u>s</u>it
τ	tau	*t* as in <u>t</u>oe
υ	upsilon	between <u>ee</u> and <u>oo</u>
φ	phi	*f* as in <u>f</u>oot
χ	chi	*ch* as in lo<u>ch</u>
ψ	psi	*ps* as in chi<u>ps</u>
ω	omega	*o* as in h<u>o</u>me

USEFUL ANCIENT GREEK WORDS, PHRASES, AND NUMBERS

English	Ancient Greek	Pronounced
Hello/Goodbye	*Khaire*	Chay-re
Thank you	*Kharis soi*	Cha-ris soy
Excuse me	*Sungignô'ske moi*	Sun-gig-know-ske moy
How can I help?	*Ti d' ou mellô?*	Ti doo mellow?
No thank you	*Ma'llista*	Mal-ist-a
Cheers! (I drink your health!)	*Propinô soi*	Pro-pee-know soy
Where?	*Pou?*	Poo?
When?	*Pote?*	Pott-eh?

Numbers	Ancient Greek
1	I
2	II
3	III
4	IIII
5	Γ
6	ΓI
7	ΓII
8	ΓIII
9	ΓIIII
10	Δ

GREAT ANCIENT GREEKS

Aesop (lived before the 6th century BC)
A slave who is said to have made up a series of stories or fables, which were later written down. Aesop was a slave on the island of Samos and may have come from an African family, but not much else is known about him.

Alexander the Great (356–23 BC)
The son of the Macedonian king, Philip II, Alexander was a famous leader, soldier, and conqueror. He became King of Macedonia when Philip was murdered in 336 BC, and like his father before him took control of most of ancient Greece. Alexander also conquered Persia and many other lands, creating a huge Greek empire. But he died at just 32 years, possibly after being poisoned.

Archimedes (around 287–12 BC)
Great scientist and inventor who studied space and physics, and invented the Archimedes screw for lifting water. He also invented many weapons to help defend Syracuse in Italy from the Romans, who eventually raided the city and killed Archimedes.

EUREKA!

Archimedes is famous for shouting "Eureka!" as he climbed into the bath. "Eureka" means "I've got it!" Archimedes had made an important discovery. So what really happened?

Archimedes saw that when he climbed into his full bathtub, some water fell out over the sides. He realised that the water he had displaced (pushed out) must take up the same volume as his body.

Then he realised that if an object is heavier than the water it displaces, it sinks. But if an object displaces an amount of water that is heavier than itself, it floats.

Aristophanes (around 445–385 BC)

Playwright from Athens who wrote mainly comedies, such as *The Frogs* and *The Birds*.

Aristotle (384–322 BC)

A scientist, philosopher, and writer, Aristotle was born in Macedonia but moved to Athens, where he was taught by Plato. During his life, Aristotle travelled a lot. He wrote about many things including animals, biology, space, weather, and literature.

Draco (7th century BC)

A dreaded leader; see box on page 8.

Euripides (around 485–06 BC)

Playwright from Athens; author of many of the most famous Greek tragedies, including *Medea* and *Electra*.

Herodotus (around 460–370 BC)

Famous historian. He was born in Ionia (a Greek colony in what is now Turkey) and later moved to Athens, then to Italy. His writings reveal a lot about ancient Greek wars, people, and culture.

Homer (probably lived sometime in the 8th century BC)

Great ancient Greek poet, author of *The Iliad*, about the Trojan War, and *The Odyssey*, about the hero Odysseus's journey home from the war. He is said to have been born on the island of Chios, and according to legend he was blind. In Homer's day, poets recited their poems – they were only written down much later.

Pausanias (lived during the 2nd century AD)

A Greek tourist and writer who went all over ancient Greece and wrote a book called *The Description of Greece* about what he saw.

Pericles (around 495–429 BC)

Political leader who controlled Athens from 443–429 BC. He had the Parthenon temple built in Athens and made many new laws.

Plato (427–347 BC)

Athenian philosopher who studied politics and power. In his youth Plato was a follower of Socrates. After Socrates' death, Plato left Athens, but he later returned and started a school called The Academy.

Pythagoras (around 580–500 BC)

Philosopher and mathematician who lived in Croton, a Greek colony in Italy. He led a band of followers in a mystical cult, and also made several important mathematical discoveries.

Sappho (around 610–550 BC)

A famous poet, Sappho is famous for her short, beautiful love poems – though only a few pieces of her work survive.

Socrates (469–399 BC)

Great philosopher of Athens who questioned power, religion, and morality (right and wrong). Socrates did not write books, but discussed ideas with his friends and followers in Athens, who later wrote them down. A court in Athens sentenced Socrates to death for teaching his ideas to the young people of Athens.

Sophocles (around 496–405 BC)

An Athenian playwright famous for his tragedies, such as *Oedipus Rex* and *Antigone*. Sophocles was the first writer to use three actors.

ANCIENT GREECE AT A GLANCE

TIMELINE

(Note: dates given are approximate.)

BEFORE 3000 BC PREHISTORIC GREECE

40,000 BC	The area that will become ancient Greece is home to early cave people.
6000 BC	People settle on the island of Crete.
5000 BC	Mediterranean peoples begin farming (instead of just hunting and gathering food).
4000 BC	People settle on the Greek islands.

3000–1100 BC THE BRONZE AGE

3000 BC	The Minoan civilization develops on the island of Crete.
1600 BC	Mycenaean culture grows on mainland Greece.
1450 BC	The Mycenaeans dominate Greece and destroy Minoan palaces.
1250 BC	The Mycenaeans fight the Trojan War against Troy.
1200 BC	Many Greeks leave Greece and settle in other lands.
1100 BC	Mycenaean culture declines.

1100–800 BC THE DARK AGE

During this time, Greek culture declines and the art of writing is lost.

800–500 BC THE ARCHAIC PERIOD

The word archaic means "old".

800 BC	The ancient Greeks start using a new writing system.
776 BC	Date of the first recorded Olympic Games.
700 BC	Greeks set up colonies around the Mediterranean.
621 BC	Draco writes a strict set of new laws for the city of Athens.
600 BC	Coins are used in Greece for the first time.
546 BC	The Persians start to invade and conquer parts of Greece.
507 BC	Athenian leader Cleisthenes introduces early democracy.

500–323 BC	THE CLASSICAL PERIOD
490 BC	The Greeks defeat Persia at the Battle of Marathon.
479 BC	The Greeks beat the Persians and kick them out of Greece.
449 BC	Greece and Persia make a peace pact.
440–430 BC	Athens is at the height of its "golden age" of culture.
445 BC	Athens makes a peace deal with its neighbour Sparta.
431–404 BC	Peloponnesian Wars between Athens and Sparta.
430–426 BC	An outbreak of the plague hits Athens and Sparta.
404 BC	Sparta finally defeats and conquers Athens.
395–340 BC	Battles between Sparta and other Greek city-states.
338 BC	King Philip II of Macedonia takes over most of Greece.
336–423 BC	Alexander the Great, Philip's son, rules Greece and conquers Persia and many other lands.

323–30 BC	THE HELLENISTIC AGE

The period of history before the Romans took over ancient Greece.

323–148 BC	After Alexander's death, the Greek city-states fight each other.
Around 200 BC	The Romans begin to attack and invade Greece.
146 BC	The Romans rule most of Greece.

FURTHER READING

BOOKS

Eyewitness: Ancient Greece, Anne Pearson (Dorling Kindersley, 2004)

Horrible History: The Groovy Greeks, Terry Deary (Scholastic, 1995)

The Usborne Internet-linked Encyclopedia of Ancient Greece, Lesley Miles (Usborne, 2003)

WEBSITES

- BBC Schools, Ancient Greece:
  www.bbc.co.uk/schools/ancientgreece/main_menu.shtml
- History for Kids, Ancient Greece:
  www.historyforkids.org/learn/greeks/

GLOSSARY

acropolis part of a city built on a high hill and surrounded by strong walls; the word means "high town"

agora flat, open meeting-place or marketplace in a town centre

anaesthetic painkiller used during operations

architect someone who designs buildings

artisan someone who makes things; a craftsperson

Assembly public meeting where citizens can vote on state decisions

chariot kind of cart pulled by an animal

chorus band of 12–15 men who act like a narrator in a Greek play; they all speak at the same time and may also sing and dance together

citizen in ancient Greece, a full member of society, who can vote and own property

city-state independent state made up of a city and the land and villages around it. Each city-state has its own rulers and laws.

civilization complex society with cities, art, and culture

Classical period period in Greek history usually said to last from about 500–323 BC (Alexander the Great's death)

colony place that has been taken over and run by another country

crater bowl-shaped hollow left by a big explosion

democracy rule by the people, from the Greek words *demos* meaning people and *kratos* meaning power

drachma the basic unit of currency in ancient Greece

gymnasium kind of leisure centre where men can exercise and chat

jury members of the public who vote on whether someone standing trial is innocent or guilty

laurels leaves and branches of the laurel plant

magistrate type of judge

mythology ancient stories about gods, heroes, and how the world began

navigator someone who finds the way on a journey

oracle religious shrine where people can go to ask the gods questions

philosophy study of the nature of the world, things, and ideas,

sacrifice to give something up, for example as a gift to the gods

scytale stick used to make coded messages, by writing on to a strip of leather wrapped around the stick

sexist treating people unfairly on the basis of whether they are male or female

shrine sacred or special place built in honour of a god or great person

siege attack on a city or building, made by surrounding it and imprisoning the people inside

tactics decisions and actions made to try to win a battle or influence a situation

tapestry picture or pattern made by weaving coloured threads into cloth

tectonic plate large sections that make up the Earth's outer crust

terrace row of houses that are joined together, rather than standing alone

tomb place where people are buried, especially in ancient times

tragedy type of play dealing with serious and sad events

trance strange state that a person can enter, where they seem distracted by their thoughts and unable to see or hear

tyrant ruler who has complete control, often after seizing power

underclass poorest people in a society, such as beggars, the unemployed, and low-paid workers

INDEX